BRIT___
MOTORCYCLES
OF THE 1960s AND '70s

Mick Walker

SHIRE PUBLICATIONS

Published in Great Britain in 2018 by Shire Publications,
part of Bloomsbury Publishing Plc
PO Box 883, Oxford, OX1 9PL, UK
1385 Broadway, 5th Floor, New York, NY 10018, USA
Email: shire@shirebooks.co.uk   www.shirebooks.co.uk

A CIP catalogue record for this book is available from the
British Library.

Shire Library no. 654   •   ISBN-13: 978 0 74781 057 5

Mick Walker has asserted his right under the Copyright,
Designs and Patents Act, 1988, to be identified as the
author of this book.

Designed by Tony Truscott Designs, Sussex, UK
Typeset in Perpetua and Gill Sans.
Printed in China through World Print Ltd.

18 19 20   13 12 11 10 9 8 7 6 5

COVER IMAGE
Design and photography by Peter Ashley. Front cover:
1966 Triumph Bonneville T120, with grateful thanks to
Tom Harris. Back cover detail: National Benzole petrol
pump globe emblem, collection of Tom Harris.

TITLE PAGE IMAGE
The long-established AMC (Associated Motor Cycles) had
its origins back in 1901, when the Collier family produced
their first Matchless machine for sale. But by the beginning
of the 1960s AMC's problems were mounting. The bike
shown is a 1962 Matchless G2CSR two-fifty.

CONTENTS PAGE IMAGE
The 1961 Matchless 31 CSR 650cc.

Shire Publications is supporting the Woodland Trust, the UK's leading woodland conservation charity, by funding the dedication of trees.

CONTENTS

INTRODUCTION

I<small>N</small> 1959 British registrations of motorcycles reached a record of 331,806 machines, a figure that, regrettably, would never be achieved again. The British motorcycle industry seemed blissfully unaware of what the 1960s held in store for it. Warning signs had already begun to appear, such as the participation of the Japanese Honda works team in the Isle of Man TT races for the first time in June 1959, and the debut of an inexpensive small car, the Mini, but the industry's management took no real action.

Then there were the social changes. Following the end of the Second World War, large numbers of new housing estates had been constructed, together with factories, offices and other places of work. This rapid expansion had meant that for the first time many workers now had to travel considerable distances to their places of employment, and so personal transport became a big issue, as many of the new housing estates were not served by railways or bus routes. Before the war the humble pedal cycle had been a vital means of travelling the often short distance from home to work. But now the bicycle rapidly fell out of fashion, largely because, as journey distances, and wages, increased, mechanised transport became all-important. During the 1950s this usually meant two wheels – either a moped, a scooter or a motorcycle. Also during the 1950s there had been credit squeezes, petrol rationing (due to the Suez crisis), and variations in the rate of purchase tax (the forerunner of VAT).

But by the end of the 1950s the vast majority of restrictions had been lifted – and so came the record sales figures achieved in 1959. However, what many did not take into account at the time was that almost half of these sales were of imported (European) models, mainly mopeds, scooters and ultra-lightweight motorcycles. Although this was at the low-value end of the market, it was a portion of the industry that represented potential future expansion, but which, sadly, the British manufacturers chose largely to ignore. The new customers tended to progress naturally from a moped to a scooter, and finally to a motor car, as soon as their finances allowed.

During the late 1950s and early 1960s the scooter sector was the focus of a vibrant social scene. The scooter importers, led by Lambretta and Vespa,

Opposite:
Norton's 750 Atlas used the same basic engine as the Commando model. This photograph was taken in Kent and dates from 1967.

A March 1961 Ariel advertisement showing the range of twin-cylinder two-stroke models: Arrow, Leader, and Arrow Super Sports.

had been quick to encourage this, by fostering club runs, rallies and even competitive events. By contrast, the established motorcycle clubs were run by enthusiasts for enthusiasts, and did little to encourage new customers.

The Mini (soon to be followed by a range of other new small cars from rival manufacturers) almost overnight dealt a death blow to the previously popular sidecar outfit. It could be purchased for little more than the cost of a new large-capacity motorcycle, provided four-seat saloon-car comfort, and was also fun to drive, thanks to its excellent roadholding and cornering abilities. For the family, it provided all-year weather protection, something the traditional motorcycle sidecar combination was unable to match.

As the 1960s began, few people in Europe, or for that matter North America, had much knowledge of Japan, and they had even less idea of the challenge its motorcycle industry was capable of providing. But, as described in a later chapter, the Japanese, led by Honda, Suzuki and Yamaha, in a few years caused the once great British motorcycle industry to go into terminal decline.

The 650 Triumph Bonneville was the most popular British sports roadster of the 1960s; it was also very successful in long-distance endurance racing.

Brochure for the popular Norton Dominator 88 Sports Special; it won its class at the 1962 1,000-km production race at Silverstone and was also the class winner at that year's Thruxton 500-mile race.

Below: View of the BSA Small Heath factory production line during the mid-1960s. Machines are the 654cc Lightning twin-carburettor sports model.

The domestic British industry did not seem to appreciate the dangers it faced as it entered the decade that was to become known as the 'Swinging Sixties'. It failed to realise that the Japanese would not be content in the long term to build and market only small-capacity machines, and the beginning of the end for the British motorcycle industry came in 1965 with the launch of the Honda CB450, soon nicknamed the 'Black Bomber'. The threat from four-wheeled vehicles was also not fully realised, and another threat was the legislation being introduced by the British government to restrict new riders to a maximum of 250cc. This was a result of the large increase in learner riders during the 1959 sales boom; unfortunately, the big leap in sales had been matched by a correspondingly large jump in accidents. Yet another problem was the bad press caused by the rivalry between so-called 'Rockers' and 'Mods', described in the next chapter.

Below: The first series production British bike with five speeds, the Royal Enfield 250 Super 5, 1963.

CAFÉ RACER CULTURE

THE 'CAFÉ RACER' was a phenomenon of the 1960s – but not exclusively. The antics of leather-jacketed British youth during the Swinging Sixties were reflected, though in a much smaller way, in two other eras: that of the 'Promenade Percys' in the 1930s, and the intense but short-lived American love affair with the café racer during the 1970s. In all three eras, the machines and their owners were seen very much as rebels against the motorcycling establishment.

The first coming of the café racer was during the 1930s, when the world was slowly emerging from the Great Depression. After years of gloom, there was at long last enough money for most youngsters to get a motorcycle. Their new-found enthusiasm resulted in many of them making collective runs to the coast (hence the 'Promenade Percy' tag) or taking advantage of the recently constructed trunk roads built after the First World War, such as the Cambridge and Southend arterial highways from London. But Hitler's war put a stop to all forms of civilian motorcycling, and the friendly pre-war rivalries on the King's Highway were replaced with battles of a more earnest and perilous nature. And after the end of the conflict in 1945 it was many years before post-war Britain was able to throw off the yoke of austerity and finally discard the ration books.

Various events combined to bring about the rebirth of the café racer, together with the advent of the 'Rocker' – and subsequently 'Mod' – cults. New motorcycles, such as the BSA Gold Star and Star twins, the Norton Dominator, the Royal Enfield Meteor and Constellation, the Triumph Tiger 110 and Bonneville, and the Velocette Venom created a new breed of rider, while films such as Marlon Brando's *The Wild Ones* expressed, albeit in somewhat extreme form, the concept of biker as rebel. Add to this the potency of the greatest of all pop music phenomena, rock 'n' roll, increasing affluence, and the mushrooming 'youth culture', and the ingredients were all in place.

Yet another vital factor in the post-war rise of the café racer was the attempt by many motorcycle owners to replicate the pukka racers seen on

Opposite:
One man's café racer, essentially a Matchless G80 Scrambler with all-alloy engine, lightweight frame, 5-gallon alloy tank, disc front brake, high-level exhaust and clip-on handlebars (which attach individually to the top of each of the forks rather than forming one continuous handlebar).

A BSA A10 six-fifty café racer. Although the basic engine and frame are original, just about everything else has been changed or modified.

A 1967 shot of a 692cc Royal Enfield Constellation (left) and a 349cc Velocette Viper (right). Both bikes were popular with the café racer fraternity.

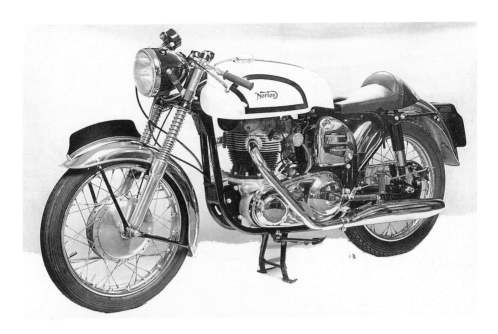

British short circuits. During the late 1950s, and even more so in the early 1960s, the aspiring café racer almost invariably opted for a machine styled after those to be seen at race circuits such as Brands Hatch and Silverstone. At the same time, certain manufacturers, notably BSA and Velocette, built limited numbers of 'clubman racers', which, though originally conceived for track use, more often than not found their way on to the public highway.

A Norton 750 Atlas with all the café racer fittings, including racing tank and single seat, rear-sets, clip-ons and swept-back exhaust header pipes.

These bikes, together with many owner-converted standard production machines, formed the nucleus of the era's 'ton-up' fraternity. Road-racing equipment, such as lightweight aluminium or glass-fibre petrol and oil tanks, low-slung clip-on handlebars, rearset foot controls and the like, soon became essential items – and, for their suppliers, a highly lucrative business. Many a Rocker was to make a successful switch from the street to the race circuit, among them Peter Ferbrache, Dave Croxford, Rex Butcher, Bill Ivy, the

Rider's view of a Norton Dominator café racer, showing the fuel tank, clip-ons, and matching rev counter/ speedometer.

Typical café scene from the 1960s. Machines are a mixture, including Norton, Triumph, BSA and a solitary Honda.

customising master Paul Dunstall, sprint star John Hobbs, and even the author himself.

Many of these speed stars spent the early part of their motorcycling careers in all-night transport cafés and coffee bars ('coffee bar cowboys' was another name for the breed), sipping frothy cups of espresso coffee to the blare of rock 'n' roll from a brightly lit jukebox. To alleviate the boredom, they devised a ritual of daredevil, death-defying sprints from one café or coffee bar to the next. Another craze was the out-of-town 'burn-up' – on the way to spectate at a race meeting, for example. Many of the cafés and coffee bars have become legendary, most notably the Ace Café on London's

North Circular Road, but also including the Busy Bee on the Watford Bypass, and Johnsons on the A20 near Brands Hatch in Kent.

The motorcycles themselves included converted series-production factory-manufactured bikes that were customised and tuned by their owners, but also a host of specials, the best-known being the Triton (Triumph engine, Norton frame). Most of these bikes, of both kinds, were surprisingly basic, certainly in terms of engine tuning. They may have looked radically different, but the performance of the typical 1960s café racer was never developed much from its original concept. Lightly tuned, production-based street bikes, they were the playthings of youngsters in their late teens or early twenties, bent on snatching their share of high-speed thrills and spills before the time arrived to grow up and settle down. Apart from minor engine modifications and the bolting-on of over-the-counter accessories, the typical café racers of the 1960s were surprisingly standard: there were no paint artists with airbrushes, no tank murals or glittering metal-flake or candy paint jobs, few expanses of chrome plate, no custom shows, nor even organised club runs.

But what there was in abundance was comradeship. Although there was no real café racer organisation, there was eventually a place where like-minded individuals could meet in a different setting. This was the London-based Fifty-Nine Club. The driving force behind this venture was

Triton with Wideline Norton frame, pre-unit Triumph engine, Roadholder front forks and 2-leading shoe front brake.

the late Father Bill Shergold – an enthusiastic motorcyclist himself. The typical uniform of the 1960s Rocker was a black leather jacket, boots with white socks showing over the top, and either pudding-basin or jet (space) helmet, plus leather gloves. Most wore goggles, many of them the racing type.

Cafés and coffee bars were the Rockers' traditional meeting place. Unlike in today's profit-driven world, there was no obligation to purchase more than a single cup of espresso coffee, no matter how long one stayed, and there were usually the low-cost attractions of bar billiards and a jukebox stacked with the latest rock 'n' roll hits. In many ways these venues were ideal, being not only cheap, but, mercifully, not licensed to sell alcohol. But by the following decade, as people became more affluent and other crazes took over, the transport café and coffee bar venues all but ceased to exist.

The so-called 'Mods' were the parallel movement to the Rockers. To the chagrin of motorcyclists, Mods rode scooters, largely Lambretta or Vespa models. Over the period from about 1960 to 1965, the Mods transformed their scooters from highly ornamented machines with lashings of chrome plate, masses of extra lights, spare wheels, mirrors and even handlebar tassles,

Another popular home-brewed special was the Norvin, this time with a 1,000cc Vincent V-twin engine and Norton chassis.

to stripped-down creations whose frames were bereft of almost any bodywork whatsoever. The installation of noisy sports silencers was mandatory, and, instead of outright performance, the scooterist's aspiration was to corner his machine with the footboards raising sparks against the tarmac.

Inevitably, rivalry between Mods and Rockers ran high, with battles being fought on the seafronts of Brighton, Southend-on-Sea, Great Yarmouth and other English coastal resorts. The British media enjoyed a frenzy of indignation, seizing on the Mod-versus-Rocker battles with a glee that no amount of synthetic moral outrage could disguise. Scarcely a summer weekend passed without reports of clashes on the seafront, terrified locals, irate shopkeepers and overstretched police. The reality was somewhat different to the image created by the sensational headlines in the press. There were some problems, but not to the extent that the media would have had their readers believe.

There are still scooter rallies today, notably in Great Yarmouth, and an annual Rockers' reunion in Brighton, while the Ace Café has become a national institution. The 'battles' of the past are all but forgotten on both sides, as the aggressive high spirits of youth have given way to moderate, middle-aged nostalgia.

A Gus Kuhn Norton 750 Commando café racer.

THE RISING SUN

VIRTUALLY UNNOTICED in the West, the Japanese between 1945 and 1959 created a vast motorcycle industry, which had concentrated almost exclusively upon their home market. However, at the start of the 1960s, this huge industry was ready to take on the world. Led by Honda, the Japanese manufacturers made their international debut, more or less simultaneously, on the racing circuit and in the showroom.

When they first appeared in Europe and North America, Japanese racing bikes were only moderately successful. Similarly, their production street bikes appeared somewhat strange to the Western eye, although technically innovative and loaded with standard features that would have cost extra for on British machines.

Within a few years, however, this situation had changed drastically. Not only was almost every class of Grand Prix racing dominated by the Japanese, but also such firms as Honda, Bridgestone (known today as a major tyre manufacturer), Suzuki, Hodaka, Kawasaki and Yamaha were becoming well-respected names in both Europe and North America, enjoying the strongest dealer network in the industry.

So what had caused such a major reversal of fortunes? First, the Japanese had created a firm foundation within their domestic market, which by the end of the 1950s was one of the strongest and fastest-growing in the world. Next, they had planned a properly funded export drive, which included a substantial racing budget. In addition, they had recruited the right people in the various countries they had targeted for their sales invasion. Never in the history of motorcycling had one nation achieved such dramatic inroads into worldwide markets in so little time, and with such determination and efficiency.

But this was no mere marketing exercise. There were good reasons behind the Japanese success story. Without exception, Japanese motorcycles featured an all-round excellence that neither European nor American manufacturers could match. Their strong performance, good build quality and high level of technical refinement, plus the all-important value for

Opposite:
The Honda stand at the London Earls Court Show, November 1964.

17

British imports of Honda machines began at the beginning of the 1960s, including this 1961 C92 overhead-camshaft twin. Styling was strange to western eyes.

A Honda CB72 Super Sports in an American showroom in 1962; in the background is a British Matchless G80CS. Already the Japanese were beginning to make a serious sales challenge to the long-established British marques.

money, combined to present a winning formula. They could be faulted only in the handling and roadholding departments, deficiencies that were mainly due to 'pogo-like' rear suspension units and inferior tyre compounds.

After the Second World War Japan was a shattered country, with most of its factories and cities in ruins. However, amazingly, within a few years, an economic and industrial miracle emerged from this desolation. By 1952 a peak of around 120 marques had been recorded, but few survived until the

A typical Japanese motorcycle of the mid-1950s. German influence is clearly visible.

late 1950s. Those that did were headed by Honda, Suzuki and Yamaha. Others that were still operational as the 1960s began included Meguro (later swallowed up by Kawasaki), Tohatsu, Pointer, Bridgestone, Liner, Lilac and Rabbit.

One man more than any other is seen today to have been the driving force behind the rise and ultimate success of the Japanese motorcycle industry – Soichiro Honda. Born on 17 November 1906, he was the son of a blacksmith in Komyo, now part of modern-day Hamamatsu. From an early age he showed a great interest in anything mechanical and at school displayed a leaning towards practical matters. After serving an apprenticeship as a car mechanic, he opened his own garage in the early 1930s and did well enough to take up car racing. This ended abruptly, however, after a serious accident in 1936. He sold the business and began manufacturing piston rings. Towards the end of the war, his factory was heavily bombarded, and after the conflict he sold out to Toyota, taking a year off.

In October 1946 Honda set up the impressive-sounding Honda Technical Research Institute. In reality, this was little more than a wooden hut on a levelled bomb site on the outskirts of Hamamatsu. After the war the Japanese were in dire need of personal transport, provided it was cheap, and Honda had discovered a cache of five hundred small engines (intended for military generators). By adapting these tiny power units and fitting them

Soichiro Honda in 1968 with the ten-millionth motorcycle produced by his company, a CB450 twin.

Opposite: Honda workers on the production line, c. 1961.

to conventional pedal cycles, Soichiro Honda had taken his first step towards becoming the world's largest motorcycle manufacturer, a position his company was to achieve in little more than fifteen years.

Soon he was overwhelmed with orders and the stock of engines dwindled rapidly. So, to meet demand, he set out to design and build a petrol engine of his own. The result was the 49cc, two-stroke, single-cylinder engine, coded Type A, which first appeared during 1947. When the Honda Motor Company was incorporated in September 1948, the Type A had obtained an impressive 60 per cent share of the Japanese home market.

The Type E, introduced in mid-1951, was Honda's first four-stroke motorcycle. This featured an unusual three-valve arrangement (two inlet, one exhaust) and two carburettors. Although the newcomer set a new record for Japanese motorcycle production of 130 units per day, Honda was not without problems: for example, in 1953 he was almost forced out of business because of cash-flow issues, but he was saved by his bank.

The most successful powered two-wheeler of all time, the Honda 'Step-Thru', began with the C100 Super Cub in 1958, with flywheel magneto ignition.

Honda's big breakthrough occurred in 1958, with the debut of the C100 Super Cub 'Step-Thru' commuter bike. Introduced in October that year, it sold in vast numbers: production in 1959, for example, reached an incredible 755,589 machines. Equipped with a 50cc four-stroke overhead-valve engine, the Cub at long last achieved something that many manufacturers had attempted but none had yet delivered – a motorcycle for 'everyman'. Until this time, the world's motorcycle builders, including

the British industry, had largely concentrated on what could be described as enthusiast models – which effectively limited mass sales. Honda's approach was different, shown by its advertising slogan – 'You meet the nicest people on a Honda'. By 1983 a staggering 15 million Super Cubs had been sold worldwide, outselling any other powered two-wheeler many times over. As one commentator later put it, 'the Honda was to motorcycling what Hoover was to vacuum cleaners'.

Soichiro Honda – and indeed all of the Japanese motorcycle industry – had a very good approach to the market. For example, in 1954 Honda visited Europe, taking in the best of the industry, including NSU in Germany (then the leading manufacturer of mopeds and small motorcycles, and world champions in the lightweight classes of Grand Prix racing), and Great Britain, and even the Isle of Man TT races. Honda also spent heavily on testing his products in competition, and on research and development.

Unfortunately, at the same time during the late 1950s and early 1960s, the British industry was resting on its laurels. What money was earned was going to shareholders, rather than funding research and developing brand-new models. BSA, the biggest British manufacturing group, comprising not only the parent company but also Triumph, Ariel and Sunbeam, was at that time led by Edward Turner (managing director of the automotive division) and Eric Turner (no relation).

A 1964 Honda CB92. Its 125cc twin-cylinder engine put out 15 bhp at 10,500 rpm, giving a maximum speed of 81 mph.

In August Edward Turner travelled to Japan to study the industry there, which was reputedly producing 62,000 motorcycles per month. Even before he left, Turner knew that Japan posed a serious threat. Yet after his return nothing seemed to change. Was it arrogance or incompetence, or a mixture of both? It seems that Turner was the wrong man for the job. He was then on the verge of retirement. The mission required a younger, less biased individual. As it was, the warning went largely unheeded.

View of the controls and instrumentation for the Honda CB72/77 series. Note features such as combined speedometer and rev counter, twin mirrors, steering damper knob and electric start button (extreme right).

The Honda CB450 double overhead-camshaft twin came as an unpleasant surprise to the British motorcycle industry, which had previously hoped that the CB77 350cc twin would be Honda's limit.

An early pre-production Honda CB750 outside the American importer's headquarters in Gardena, early 1969.

Honda's CBX 1000 aped the Japanese company's amazing 250/297cc six-cylinder Grand Prix racers. It went on sale in 1978 as the marque's top-of-the-range sports tourer.

Throughout the 1960s and 1970s the Japanese forged ahead, introducing vast numbers of motorcycles. By the 1970s, just four manufacturers were left: Honda, Kawasaki, Suzuki and Yamaha.

Honda gradually progressed from models such as the 125cc CB92, 250cc CB72 and 305cc CB77 in the early 1960s, the CB450, and finally the CB750 as that decade unfolded. Then in the 1970s came the CB360, a series of fours, including the CB400F and CB500, and finally the GL1000 Gold Wing flat-four and the breathtaking CBX1000 six.

Kawasaki were largely two-stroke in the 1960s, before finally embracing the superbike era with the H2 750cc triple two-stroke and the 900cc ZI double overhead-camshaft four, both of which arrived during the early 1970s.

Suzuki built a range of two-strokes from 50cc to 750cc until the end of the 1970s, plus the RE5 Rotary (Wankel), before finally switching to four-strokes in various capacities from 370cc to 1,000cc by the end of the 1970s.

Like Suzuki, Yamaha stuck to two-strokes until the late 1970s; these later machines included the XS650 twin, the XS750 triple and the XS1100 four, the 750 and 1100 both featuring shaft final drive.

All this successful activity in the motorcycle business enabled the four Japanese marques to branch into other areas, notably automobiles (Honda and Suzuki).

A 1966 Suzuki B105P, an early version of what would become a successful on/off-road 'green lanes' motorcycle.

THE DAWN OF THE SUPERBIKE

THE ERA of the modern superbike began at the end of the 1960s. The first such machine, the Norton Commando, arrived in the autumn of 1967, followed a year later by the debut of the BSA Rocket 3 and Triumph Trident three-cylinder models. Unfortunately for the British industry, the mighty Japanese concern Honda chose to launch its own superbike, the CB750, at the Tokyo Show in October 1968, and, unlike the overhead-valve twin-cylinder Norton and the three-cylinder BSA/Triumph models, the new Honda was equipped with a four-cylinder overhead-camshaft engine, five speeds, electric start and disc front brake.

But the Norton was the first of the new breed and it went on to establish a firm position in the superbike field, both on the street and in racing events around the world. It enjoyed a ten-year production run and helped re-establish the Norton brand.

THE NORTON COMMANDO

The Commando, and the BSA and Triumph triples, were the last mass-production, large-capacity motorcycles to be offered by the 'old' British bike industry, which by the late 1960s was coming to an end. The new Norton made its public debut at the 1967 London Earls Court Show under its new company name, Norton Villiers, which was backed by Manganese Bronze, with former car-racer Dennis Poore at the helm. Norton Villiers had taken over both AMC (Associated Motor Cycles) and the Villiers engine-manufacturing concern.

Back in January 1967 Poore had appointed Dr Stefan Bauer, formerly with Rolls-Royce, to lead a new design team at Norton Villiers; his brief was to create a new, large-displacement sports bike, but, operating on a strict budget, his team would have to use the existing Atlas-type overhead-valve parallel twin engine (this having itself been developed from the Dominator unit). Bauer had two key men in his development team: Bob Twigg, who took on the job of styling the new bike; and Bernard Hooper, who turned Bauer's drawings into actual motorcycles.

Opposite:
The BSA version of the Triumph/BSA triple had its cylinders inclined forward by some 15 degrees. This was partly a marketing ploy, and partly to help differentiate the BSA from the Triumph Trident.

Chrome headlamp and Smith's speedometer and rev counter from the 1968 Norton 750 Commando.

The Norton Commando was the first of the modern superbike class, introduced at the end of 1967.

By June 1967 the team had a prototype running on the street, and in September the Commando made its bow at Earls Court. To counter the inherent vibration found in larger parallel twins, Bauer and his team came up with a clever remedy: they mounted the 745cc Atlas engine, together with the AMC transmission and final drive, swinging arm and rear wheel, as a single, separate rubber-mounted unit. Patented under the name 'Isolastic', this allowed the power train to oscillate in a newly designed, single top tube frame, with the rider insulated from the vibrations by its flexible mounting block.

Another major difference compared to what had gone before was that the engine was canted forwards several degrees from the vertical, and a totally new frame adopted. At the time there were many who questioned the need for the latter, as the old Featherbed frame had always been seen as the Norton twin's best feature. However, as Bauer and his team realised, a new frame was needed, not only to help solve the vibration problems, but also to create a new image.

From the start, it was evident to everyone connected with the Commando project that they had a winner on their hands. It was virtually

new, available quickly, and affordable. It also looked the part and had plenty of performance. The Commando came as a ray of hope in a bleak situation. While BSA, Triumph, Velocette and Royal Enfield were all struggling to survive, the new Norton was selling rapidly in both Britain and North America.

Proving how popular the Commando became, *Motor Cycle News* readers voted it their 'Machine of the Year' on a record five occasions from 1968 until 1972. But the Commando was not only well liked by the public, it was a commercial success too. Although it appeared very different from the machines it replaced, many of its component parts were actually the same, so that not only were development costs much lower than they would have been for an all-new design, but profitability was also that much greater. Also the Norton Villiers marketing team were clever, as they were able to produce

The 745cc overhead-valve parallel twin engine from the Commando.

The clever part of the Commando was the wide range of models from one basic design. The one shown here is the 750 Interstate from the early 1970s. Note the large-capacity fuel tank and disc front brake.

The limited-production John Player Norton version took its name from the successful race team, which used special Commando machines.

a succession of variants; these included the R (Roadster) Fastback, S (Sportster) Production Racer, Chopper, Interpol (police motorcycle) and Interstate. An 850–829cc model was introduced in 1973, and by 1975 it had been given an electric start and left-hand gearchange. The final batch of thirty Commando machines (850s) was built in 1978.

The 850 (829cc) Commando.

A police version of the Commando, the 750 Interpol, was used by a number of British forces during the 1970s.

TRIUMPH TRIDENT AND BSA ROCKET 3

The Triumph Trident and its close relative the BSA Rocket 3 took almost half a decade to transfer from drawing board to metal. In retrospect this was a fatal mistake, which cost them a potential lead of several years over the opposition in what is now known as the superbike era.

Work on the new design began at Triumph's Meriden works, near Coventry, during the spring of 1964, with Doug Hele, Bert Hopwood and

Royal Enfield built the 692cc Constellation, seen here with optional air-flow fairing.

Jack Wicks all involved. The original idea was to create a 750cc-class machine from, in effect, one-and-a-half Triumph Speed Twin five-hundreds; this was an excellent concept, both as a motorcycle and from a production point of view, as many existing Triumph design features were used.

The BSA Group, which then owned Triumph, did not authorise production until 1967, thereby losing the chance to steal a march on its main commercial competitor, the Honda CB750, which arrived in the showrooms during 1969. Furthermore, it was in Formula 750 racing, rather than on the street, that the BSA/Triumph triples were to make the most impact, dominating Formula 750 events in the early 1970s.

The engine design followed conventional Triumph practice, in effect adding a third cylinder to the existing twin. Valve gear copied the pattern set by Edward Turner, with two camshafts front and rear of the cylinder block, driven by gears and operating pushrods encased by vertical tubes lying between the cylinders. Both the cylinder barrels and head were single castings of aluminium, the former with separate austenitic liners. The three-cylinder engine was (unlike the Norton Commando) a unit-construction design, which meant that the rear of the main section doubled up as the gearbox shell. However, the lubrication system was of the dry-sump variety with a separate oil tank. Initially, the ignition was by battery with three separate coils mounted in series underneath the seat.

The BSA and Triumph triples were not exactly the same. The original Tridents (including those raced by the works in Formula 750 events from 1969 to 1972) had vertical (upright) cylinders. But from the start the BSA version had its cylinders inclined forward by some 15 degrees. (Later, during the Norton Villiers Triumph era, Tridents were offered with the BSA layout – confusing for historians.) The frames were also different, whereas the front forks and wheel hubs were identical components.

Three carburettors, one per cylinder, were fitted, while the exhaust system was a three-into-four-into-two layout, as the pipe from the centre cylinder split and was connected into both the outer cylinder pipes, which then swept back into individual silencers on each side of the bike. In their early guise, these were what was termed the 'Raygun' type, for they terminated in a flat end-plate with three small outlet pipes with their ends cut off at an angle.

The styling of the BSA and Triumph triples was not universally praised at launch; their appearance could best be described as conservative.

Engine output was a claimed 58 bhp at 7,250 rpm. The first batches were exclusively for export, examples being sent primarily to Commonwealth countries, including Australia and Canada, plus the United States of America. But by early 1969 both the BSA and Triumph triples were beginning to reach the home market.

Motorcyclist Illustrated tested an example of the BSA version, which retailed for £614 3s 5d, reporting favourably on the model's overall performance. Speed, acceleration, roadholding and braking were all viewed positively. Negative comments were restricted to minor concerns about the lighting switch, the accessibility of the side (prop) stand and the effort it took the tester to operate the centre stand. He also mentioned low-speed vibration and said that the twin horns were less effective than they should have been, as they directed their notes to the rear, rather than the front. Maximum speed was approaching 125 mph.

There is no doubt that sales of the BSA Rocket 3 and the Triumph Trident were affected by the arrival of the single overhead-camshaft four-cylinder, four-stroke Honda

The engine from the 1970 Royal Enfield Interceptor Mark II.

The BSA Rocket 3 (and its close relative the Triumph Trident) took several years to transfer from drawing board to reality.

The BSA (and Triumph) triples were successful not only in the showroom but on the race track too, with victories at the very top level.

CB750 and, to a lesser extent, of another Japanese challenger, the Kawasaki HI 500cc two-stroke triple. Neither oriental bike possessed the handling and roadholding of the British bikes, but the Honda in particular had a level of sophistication that no other mass-produced motorcycle could match in 1969. Despite this competition – and the success of their British competitor, the Norton Commando – the BSA and Triumph triples eventually went on to sell in considerable numbers both at home and abroad. However, had they appeared earlier, these figures would probably have been significantly higher.

The final version of the triple was the Triumph T160, which arrived at the beginning of 1975; production ended later that year.

The BSA Group experienced financial problems during the early 1970s, and by the end of 1971 the Rocket 3 was one of only four BSA models still available for sale. Although this was to signal the end for the BSA triple, the Triumph version continued for some years.

In late 1972 a specially styled model, the X75 Hurricane, made its debut at the London Earls Court Motorcycle Show. This used the BSA version of the three-cylinder engine with a five-speed gearbox mounted in the Trident frame. With styling by the American Craig Vetter, it caused much press comment and, although mainly intended for the United States market, the Hurricane had a British list price of £895 – compared with £761 for the Honda CB750. In 1980 the motorcycle author Roy Bacon wrote: 'The styling theme [of the Hurricane] was vaguely chopperesque and the forks were extended, which increased the wheelbase to sixty inches.'

From mid-1972 the Trident was given the five-speed gearbox; with revised styling, including a more conventional exhaust system and a disc front brake, it went on sale as the T150V. In the autumn of 1973 came the blockade of the Triumph Meriden works and the birth of the Workers' Co-operative. Trident production stopped at Meriden but continued in the old BSA factory at Small Heath, Birmingham. Then in spring 1975 came the final variant, the T160. This was based on the BSA version of the triple with the cylinders sloping forward. But, unlike the BSA, it came with a five-speed gearbox. The exhaust system was also changed, as was the tank styling. For the first time a rear disc brake was specified, the same size as that fitted to the front of the existing T150V.

At the very end of 1975 the last Triumph Trident left Small Heath works, bringing down the curtain on a machine that had won the respect of owners and rival manufacturers alike.

SPECIALIST
MANUFACTURERS

A SIGNIFICANT feature of the British motorcycle industry of the 1960s and 1970s was the arrival and success of small, specialist manufacturers, in stark contrast to the decline and ultimate fall of the long-established larger firms, such as AJS, Matchless, BSA and Triumph. This new cottage industry included such names as Dunstall, Rickman, Seeley and Dresda. During the 1960s these specialists almost exclusively used British power units. However, as the 1970s unfolded they turned to Japan for their engines.

DUNSTALL

Paul Dunstall first appeared on the motorcycle scene at a Thruxton road-race meeting at Easter 1958. He was piloting his road-going Norton Dominator 99 six-hundred, which he had purchased new for £304, with full road equipment. The transformation from street bike to racer involved balancing the crankshaft and carefully reassembling the engine, but very little else. After gradually developing the machine over the next few months, which included fitting the motor into a genuine Manx Norton racing chassis, Dunstall decided to hang up his leathers and pass over the riding duties to his friend Fred Neville. An outstanding victory for the Dunstall Domiracer came during August 1961, when Neville won the main 1,000cc event at Brands Hatch.

That victory was the start of the legend, which was to feature a succession of superb Dunstall street bikes and many famous racers (though, sadly, not Neville, who was fatally injured while racing his own AJS 7R machine in the Manx Grand Prix the following month).

In January 1962 Paul Dunstall purchased most of the Domiracer motorcycles and parts, which the Norton factory had developed, including the actual machine raced by the Australian Grand Prix star Tom Phillis to a magnificent third position in the 1961 Isle of Man Senior TT. This coincided with the first Dunstall catalogue, which was full of special parts, many of which had been developed on the race track.

Opposite:
Paul Dunstall
working on one
of his famous
Domiracers in
the Brands Hatch
paddock during
1967.

Above: The top-of-the-range 1969 Dunstall 750 Atlas with twin front discs, two-into-four exhaust and full fairing.

Right: Dunstall equipment advertisement, c. 1968.

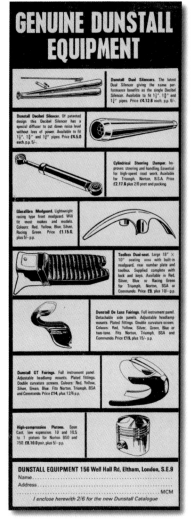

While continuing a successful race sponsorship programme, Dunstall began to expand his business further. Although specialising in Norton Dominator twins, he started offering a range of exhaust pipes and silencers for other British bikes, notably BSA and Triumph.

By 1964 he had begun selling fully modified Norton twins under the Dunstall brand name, these being available to customers at a price little more than that being asked by Norton dealers for the standard series-production model.

A typical period advertisement by Dunstall read: 'A Complete Custom service is available for Brand New Models. Machines are supplied completely fitted out with any equipment at only £25 above list price.' Customers had the chance of choosing the 88SS, 650SS or the 750 Atlas.

Together with the sale of individual components, the 'Genuine Paul Dunstall Domiracer' sales programme had begun in earnest. And with the café racer and Rocker culture just beginning to take off, so did Dunstall's sales of both parts and bikes. A new cottage industry had been born.

The most popular components were a 5.5-gallon alloy fuel tank, rev counter, rear-set footrests, shortened pillion seat or single racing saddle, clip-ons and modified headlamp brackets. The entire exhaust system was also a Dunstall speciality. There was also the chance to have a Dunstall engine tune, which on the 650SS was claimed to push maximum speed up to around 130 mph.

After road-testing one of the 650 Dunstall Dominators for the 16 June 1965 issue of *Motorcycle News*, Robin Miller wrote:

> Britain may lag behind in the space race, her brightest ideas for jet fighters may get the chop, but when it comes to producing big, beefy, mile-eating motorbikes she is supreme… I have been riding a Daddy among big bikes – the 650 Dunstall Dominator. A more magnificent, but less mean, monster I have yet to come across, in captivity that is! It took me up the A1 at a steady 100mph [there were no speed cameras then] yet trickled through stop-start Whit holiday traffic showing a dove-like side to its character which, quite honestly, I never expected.

Paul Dunstall created a successful business empire from his association with the Norton Dominator on road and track. This machine dates from the mid-1960s.

In October 1965 it was announced that, for the first time, anything other than the Norton Dominator series was to come under the Dunstall banner, and that the 1966 catalogue would feature BSA big twins, to which would shortly be added a Triumph fully kitted out in Dunstall parts.

In 1966 Dunstall branched out into first BSA (a customised Lightning is seen here), then shortly afterwards Triumph, following AMC's collapse.

Dunstall 810cc cylinder kit for Norton. The price in 1973 was £68.

So why this change in policy? For one thing, the Dunstall organisation was expanding rapidly. For another, Paul Dunstall, with his close contacts with AMC (Norton's owners), was by now in serious financial trouble.

When Norton Villiers took over the remains of AMC and launched the Commando, Dunstall was back with Norton. But he stuck with Norton a little too long, and when during the early 1970s he finally switched to Japanese

The arrival of the Commando during the late 1960s saw Dunstall adopt the new model. This is the 810 version.

machinery he became a leading exponent of the café racer craze in North America. By the middle of that decade he had established a widespread dealer network in the United States, backed up by a comprehensive sixty-page Dunstall Power Catalogue.

During the late 1970s Paul Dunstall enjoyed a close association with Suzuki, producing the classic Dunstall Suzuki GS1000 model. But then he became a victim of the recession, with its attendant drop in sales and profit. He finally sold the Dunstall brand name in 1982.

Dunstall Commando 810 Mark 2. The 1972 price was £740 plus purchase tax of £177.60.

RICKMAN

The Rickman story started before the Second World War when Ernie Rickman, father of Don and Derek, owned a garage in New Milton, Hampshire. Following their father's death in 1947, the brothers, who had both served engineering apprenticeships, ran the family garage until 1956, when they sold it to concentrate on their sporting interests. (By then they were established moto-cross riders.) In 1958 they opened a small retail shop, also in New Milton.

Next, in the search for more competitive bikes, they decided to abandon production models and construct their own. The result was a hybrid, made up from the best components available. They christened their creation 'Metisse', a French term for a female mongrel. This featured a pre-unit Triumph Tiger 100 engine, BSA frame and Norton forks, plus glass-fibre tank, seat and mudguards of their own design.

The Rickman brothers, Don and Derek, made their name with moto-cross machines such as this 649cc Triumph-engined model, mounted in the famous Metisse chassis.

A debut victory in 1959, followed by victories in the Belgian and French Grand Prix, brought requests for replica machines flooding in. So Rickman Engineering was formed and they took things a stage further by building their own lightweight frames.

Throughout the 1960s business boomed, with Triumph- and Matchless-engined Metisse models becoming the bike to have in moto-cross. Then in 1966 came the first Metisse road racers and an association with a leading racing team owner, Tom Kirby.

Their small-capacity off-road models, such as this 1972 125cc Zündapp-powered endurance bike, were a major success for Rickman Engineering in the United States.

Following its great successes in the sporting arena during the 1960s, Rickman Engineering concentrated its energies from 1970 through to 1974 on the production of lightweight moto-cross machines. More than twelve thousand were sold, mainly in the United States. In addition, several British police forces looked to Rickmans for a superior-handling motorcycle for fast patrol work. A special purpose-built police bike was designed, incorporating all the qualities for which Rickman had become world-famous. This used not only a Metisse frame, but also Rickman forks and disc brakes. Also during the early 1970s Rickman had moved into the superbike sector with the Rickman Enfield-powered seven-fifty Interceptor engine. Another superbike was the Rickman Triumph Trident.

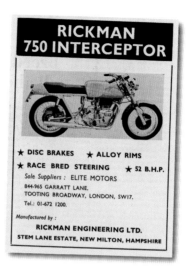

RICKMAN 750 INTERCEPTOR

★ DISC BRAKES   ★ ALLOY RIMS
★ RACE BRED STEERING   ★ 52 B.H.P.
Sole Suppliers : ELITE MOTORS
844-965 GARRATT LANE,
TOOTING BROADWAY, LONDON, SW17.
Tel.: 01-672 1200.

Manufactured by :
RICKMAN ENGINEERING LTD.
STEM LANE ESTATE, NEW MILTON, HAMPSHIRE

Rickman 750cc Interceptor superbike, March 1972.

A 1974 Rickman Enfield Interceptor. Specification included front and rear brakes, nickel-plated Metisse frame and twin Amal concentric carburettors.

By 1973 the Rickman police bike (Triumph-powered) had won favour with several forces throughout the British Isles. There was also a lightweight police mount, powered by a German 125cc Zündapp two-stroke motor.

Of the total factory output in 1974, some 90 per cent was exported to North America. This was to result in the company winning the Queen's Award for Industry. However, that same year saw the demise of the BSA Triumph group, and thus the contract to build moto-cross machines for the United States was not renewed. This left the Rickmans with the big problem of how to utilise their factory and staff. With few options left open to them, the board decided to develop the superbike concept, giving it the letters CR – Competition Replica, or was it Café Racer? Rickman switched to Japanese engines – Honda and Kawasaki. Production of the CR chassis kits soon built up to around sixty per month, while fairing production alone grew from around fifty units in 1973 to twelve thousand by 1977.

The ultimate Rickman road-burner was the 1979 Metisse Z1000 Turbocharger. Even in full street-legal guise, it was capable of a staggering performance, with 150-mph maximum and the standing quarter-mile in under ten seconds. Unfortunately, as a result of the recession and the consequent sharp downturn in demand, this was to be one of the last Metisse street bikes.

SEELEY

Colin Seeley was a sidecar racer of considerable repute during the 1960s, first with a Matchless G50-powered machine, and then a BMW Rennsport outfit. In 1965 Seeley made the business decision that was to shape his future when he purchased the manufacturing rights to AMC's racers – the AJS 7R, Matchless G50 and Manx

Former sidecar racing star Colin Seeley began motorcycle production manufacturing Matchless G50-engined racing bikes, but in the 1970s he built various Honda-engined models.

Norton (the Norton side being later sold to John Tickle). This led to the construction of several interesting machines, and not just those using AMC power units, as Seeley had at an early stage decided to update the 7R and G50 with the addition of his own specially designed frame assembly. The Seeley enterprise then entered limited production, notable for its high-quality engineering. It also manufactured its own brakes, forks and many other components, as well as the engine, gearbox and clutch assemblies.

Subsequently many other engine types were to be united with a Seeley chassis, the most notable being the QUB (Queen's University, Belfast) two-strokes of Dr Gordon Blair, the Suzuki T500 twin, and a whole succession of Honda units, including a 200cc single (for trials) and various four-cylinder units for fast road work (including the Phil Read Replica).

Like Dunstall and Rickman, Colin Seeley's business suffered with the onset of the recession at the end of the 1970s. But his skills were still in demand from such as the Brabham Formula 1 car team and the Duckhams-sponsored Crighton Norton Rotary team during the early 1990s.

DRESDA

Dave Degens began racing in the early 1960s. He then progressed to building Tritons for the café racer era, this being followed by winning the Barcelona 24-hour race (in 1965 and again in 1970). Then, into the 1970s, he embraced the new era with a succession of Japanese four-cylinder powered specials. His success in the Spanish marathon led Degens to the Paris-based Japauto concern, which commissioned the Englishman to construct an endurance racer around the Honda 750/900 engines. In 1972 this collaboration resulted in a famous victory in the Bol d'Or endurance race in France. Gérard Debrock and Roger Ruiz rode a 969cc Japauto-tuned engine housed in a Dresda chassis and weighing only 375 pounds. This success was repeated in 1973 against a vast array of factory-entered machines – a fine achievement, which firmly established the Dresda name.

Also during the 1970s Dresda constructed a number of Suzuki-powered sports roadsters, notably the GT750 three-cylinder two-stroke.

Men such as Dunstall, the Rickman brothers, Seeley and Degens showed that Great Britain had retained the ability to design and construct motorcycles that could take on and beat the best in the world.

Another small specialist British manufacturer of the 1970s was the Derby-based Silk concern, with its liquid-cooled twin-cylinder two-stroke.

SON OF BONNEVILLE

TRIUMPH TIGER 650.

Like father, like Tiger. When it comes to power and performance,
Triumph's Tiger 650 is a chip off the old champion.

Tiger's 4-stroke vertical OHV twin is a direct descendant of Bonneville's classic power plant—
the same basic engine that began winning races for Triumph some quarter of
a million bikes ago. The same engine that helped power Gene Romero to his
'71 AMA Grand National Championship.

But Tiger is fed through a single Amal 30mm concentric carburetor.
So although the engine is heavy on horses and torque, it's lighter on the gas.
And its single-carb simplicity assures clean low torque performance.

Tiger is built like "big daddy," too. With a double down tube frame that's hand-welded
for double strength. Through-The-Frame Oil System that makes an oil tank an antique.
And precision hydraulic forks, double-damped with 6-3/4" of travel.

Lightness figures big in Tiger's cat-like roadability.
It has a lightweight frame and forks, plus conical hubs that cut unsprung weight.

Triumph's Tiger 650. We call it Son of Bonneville, but it's nobody's kid brother.

ENGINE TYPE OHV-4 stroke
CYLINDERS 2
MAX. TORQUE 36.5 ft. lbs. @ 6250 rpm
BORE/STROKE 71 x 82mm
COMP. RATIO 9.1
TRANSMISSION 4-Speed gearbox
5-Speed gearbox
CARBURETOR Amal 30mm conc.
FRONT TIRE Dunlop 3.25 x 19" K70
REAR TIRE Dunlop 4.00 x 18" K70
FRONT BRAKE 8" DLS
REAR BRAKE 7" SLS
WHEEL BASE 56"
GND. CLEAR. 7"
DRY WEIGHT 386 lbs.
FUEL TANK 2½ & 3½ gals.
OIL 6 pts.

Triumph's Bonneville 650 shares many of Tiger's specs.
However, Bonneville's max. torque
is 38.5 ft. lbs. @ 6000 rpm;
it has 2 Amal 30mm concentric carbs;
and it weighs 387 pounds.

The Hot One
TRIUMPH

THE AMERICAN MARKET

During the 1960s and into the 1970s the American market was a vital one for the British motorcycle industry – and a successful one too.

Immediately after the Second World War the American economy was booming, whereas Great Britain was to suffer several years of severe austerity, including food and fuel rationing. In addition, during the late 1940s, virtually every motorcycle produced by the British industry had to go for export.

Ariel had been the first British marque to employ a full-time factory representative in the United States; that was C. E. Hopping, during 1939. Bill Johnson, himself a motorcycle enthusiast, who was to play a major role in the subsequent post-war sales boom of British bikes in the USA, had fallen in love with the Ariel Square Four and had written to Edward Turner, the designer of the machine. This was to result in Johnson becoming the Ariel (and Triumph) importer for the western seaboard of the United States in the years after the war.

Edward Turner had joined Ariel during the late 1920s, and the Square Four was launched at the end of 1930. Subsequently Turner moved to Triumph, shortly after Ariel owner Jack Y. Sangster had acquired the Triumph brand in early 1935. In mid-1937 came the launch of the famous Triumph Speed Twin, a trend-setting model designed by Turner.

After the war Edward Turner (now not merely the Triumph chief designer, but effectively managing director) went to the States, and he and Bill Johnson established a closer friendship, based on mutual respect. Before he came home, Turner offered Johnson the Triumph distribution rights for the entire United States.

By 1950, with Triumph back in full production, it was decided that the United States needed two importers, one in the west (which it already had in the shape of Johnson Motors) and one in the east – and it was here that a new company was needed. So Triumph themselves set up the Triumph Corporation, with its base in Baltimore, Maryland, and as its president they recruited an expatriate Englishman, Coventry-born Denis McCormack.

Opposite:
An August 1972
Cycle World
advertisement for
the Triumph Tiger
650, which
the American
importers
christened 'Son
of Bonneville'.

47

Above: The Triumph marque was the most popular British motorcycle in the USA during the post-Second World War era. This *Cycle World* advertisement dates from 1966.

Above right: A BSA advertisement from *Cycle* magazine in May 1965.

McCormack worked hard, and together with Bill Johnson's efforts in the west, the Triumph brand became the most successful of all British motorcycles across the Atlantic for the next three decades.

The other British marques enjoyed mixed sales fortunes in the North American market.

The BSA distribution network in the USA followed a similar line to that of Triumph, with Hap Alzina in the west and Rich Child in the east. When Edward Turner became director of the BSA Automotive Group during the 1950s, he was contracted to spend six months of each year in the USA. Sadly, he mainly concentrated on Triumph, rather than BSA. Even so, there is no doubt that Edward Turner did play a vital role in the sales and promotion of the Triumph and BSA brands in the North American market.

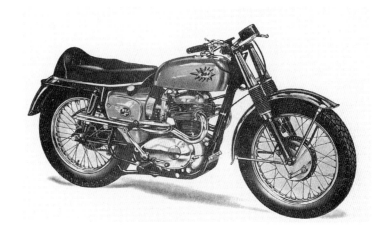

An American-only BSA 650cc Hornet for the 1966–7 model year.

Cotton was one of several small British manufacturers who exported dirt bikes to the United States during the 1960s.

In 1951 the Brockhouse Engineering Group had purchased the ailing Indian Motorcycle Company of Springfield, Massachusetts. Indian motorcycle production lasted until 1953, but Indian (i.e. Brockhouse) also acted as importers for a host of British marques during the 1950s, including

The 1968 American version of the 650cc BSA Thunderbolt, with high-rise handlebars and twin leading shoe front stopper.

A Norton advertisement from June 1960, just before Berliner became the exclusive Norton USA distributor.

Norton, Vincent, Royal Enfield, AJS and Matchless. Then in 1959 AMC acquired Brockhouse, and the Indian import activities ceased the following year. Instead, the New Jersey-based Berliner Corporation took over the imports of AMC products, including AJS, Matchless and Norton; Berliner had already gained the Norton franchise a few months earlier.

During the 1960s Berliner was to import large numbers of Nortons, though fewer AJS and Matchless, and become the second largest importer of British machines into the United States, behind BSA/Triumph.

The Berliner Corporation took its name from two brothers, Mike and Joe Berliner, the latter holding the post of President. Originally the Berliners had entered the motorcycle industry with the German Zündapp brand during the early 1950s, adding Ducati to their portfolio at the end of 1958. By the time Norton joined the family, Berliner had a ready-made and successful dealer network. It was Berliner who pressed Norton to produce its 650cc model, launched in the spring of 1961 as the Manxman (and sold from its British launch in 1962 as the 650SS).

The 1963 Norton 400 Electra was the result of a request from Berliner to provide a machine to compete with the very successful Honda CB77 305cc twin.

But even a six-fifty was not big enough for the Americans and Joe Berliner persuaded Norton to build a seven-fifty (the Atlas, in 1963), together with the 750 Scrambler (sometimes referred to as the Ranger).

From the Scrambler was developed a more serious off-roader, the P11. This was a pukka desert racer that went on to win many sporting events. The basis of the bike was a twin-carburettor Atlas engine mounted in a Matchless G85CS moto-cross chassis. Owing to what was already a lighter set of cycle parts and the wide use of aluminium, the weight was reduced by well over 40 pounds compared to the Scrambler. The P11 also sported high-level exhausts, with small lightweight mufflers. Although it was not appreciated at the time, this and the Scrambler trail bike represented an early attempt to offer a powerful, large-displacement, twin-cylinder on/off-road design, something the modern motorcycle industry was to embrace two decades later.

A September 1965 *Cycle World* advertisement for Norton's mighty 750 Atlas; again Berliner had prompted the British factory into producing this model.

From the Scrambler came the much more serious off-roader, the P11. This was a pukka desert racer, using a twin-carburettor Atlas engine mounted in a Matchless G85CS moto-cross chassis.

One must applaud Joe Berliner for coming up with the concept. Of course he knew the American market. So Berliner and the British Norton factory can well claim to have been the true pioneers of what is today a popular niche market – on both sides of the Atlantic.

After AMC folded in mid-1966, Berliner continued for a few months as the US importer. Eventually, however, the new Norton Villiers organisation set up its own American distribution network, and this coincided with the arrival of the new Commando, which, together with the BSA and Triumph triples, was the last mass-production large-capacity British motorcycle of the 'old' industry.

The Norton Villiers boss, Dennis Poore, ran a very successful advertising campaign, exclusively in the two best-selling American motorcycle magazines, *Cycle* and *Cycle World*. By pre-booking for years ahead, Poore not only reserved the inside covers but also negotiated a bargain price. This campaign kept the Commando in American buyers' sights through from the late 1960s to the mid-1970s.

Although the Commando proved a steady seller in the USA, it was Triumph and BSA which set the cash tills ringing across the Atlantic during this period. The most popular model was the Triumph Bonneville, in 650 and 750cc versions, followed by the BSA and Triumph triples, in the shape of the Rocket 3 and Trident respectively.

Norton Villiers boss Dennis Poore negotiated a special deal with the two leading American motorcycle magazines, *Cycle* and *Cycle World*, to promote the Commando model; this one dates from August 1972.

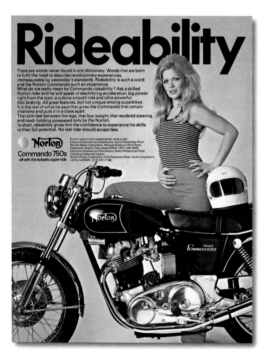

However, at the start of the 1960s the American importers were still demanding that BSA should continue building the Gold Star single. They told the British factory clearly that if they could not have the Gold Star they did not want other BSAs. And so, instead of phasing out the Gold Star, BSA had to continue production. So why was the Gold Star so much in demand? During the 1960s road racing was less popular than other branches of the sport in the United States, and Americans loved the competitive side of motorcycling. They preferred off-road, dirt-track racing to road racing on tarmac. This was exemplified by Short Track, Flat Track and TT events. The American TT event was nothing like the Isle of Man version; instead, it was a dirt-track race, with left- and right-hand turns, and a jump somewhere in the course.

The AMA (American Motorcycle Association), which formulated the rules for all branches of the sport at that time, had at the top of their tree the AMA Grand National Championship. During the 1960s this series was staged over forty-one road circuits and 145 dirt tracks. To become the Grand National Champion, a rider had to score in as many of these events as possible, both dirt and tarmac, to amass enough points to become the AMA's number one rider. The most suitable machine to embrace all these events was the BSA Gold Star.

But time stands still for no-one, and by the mid-1960s the Gold Star was no more, having finally been axed from BSA production. In its place came various BSA and Triumph twins to do battle with the American Harley-Davidsons, which were permitted to use a capacity of 750cc because they used side-valve engines, while the British challengers were limited to 500cc.

As the 1960s merged into the 1970s the AMA at last collaborated with the European-based Fédération Internationale de Motorcyclise (FIM), which controlled world motorcycle sport. This also brought about the new Formula 750 racing class, on both sides of the Atlantic.

At last British and American bikes were on equal footing – Harley-Davidson had to build an overhead-valve engine as its old side-valve advantage had been axed. Harley produced the XR750, while the British Norton (Commando), Triumph (Trident) and BSA (Rocket 3) arose to compete both in the United States and in Europe. A feature at this time was the Transatlantic Match Races. This Anglo-American contest first took place over Easter weekend 1971, and the venues were Brands Hatch, Mallory Park and Oulton Park. The first Transatlantic Match Race proved a massive success and, although staged in England, aroused considerable interest on both sides of the Atlantic.

The success of BSA, Triumph and Norton in motorcycle sport played a big part in keeping up the demand for British motorcycles in the United States. But after record exports to the USA during the late 1960s, financial difficulties were to affect the giant BSA group in the early 1970s. This meant that both BSA and Triumph models would soon be hard to find.

Although the BSA Group's problems and ultimate demise did not immediately affect sales of the Norton Commando, political events, as explained elsewhere, were to involve Norton Villiers in the problem. By the late 1970s the last Norton Commando had rolled off the production line. This marked the demise of the British motorcycle as a mainstream product not just at home, but in the United States too – a sad day indeed.

The 1970 BSA 650 Firebird street scrambler; another American market model from the Birmingham factory.

DECLINE AND FALL

FOR THE FIRST HALF of the twentieth century Great Britain led the world in motorcycle design and production. However, as the 1960s dawned, the industry went into a decline that gathered pace as the decade unfolded. Then, in the 1970s what had once been a dynamic and highly successful industry finally collapsed.

There were several reasons for this, including the emergence of the Japanese industry, the introduction of the small affordable car, and the fact that the men who had created the industry were by now old and in retirement, or dead.

This was most visible at AMC (Associated Motor Cycles). The Collier family were true pioneers of the British motorcycle industry. They began their commercial activities in Plumstead, London, during 1901, when they launched the Matchless marque. The Colliers not only designed and built these early bikes but rode them with great success, including a class victory in the very first Isle of Man TT in 1907. AMC came about as a result of the Colliers taking over a succession of rivals: AJS in 1931, Sunbeam in 1937 (later sold to BSA), Francis-Barnett in 1947, James in 1950, and finally Norton in 1953. But after the last of the Colliers, Charlie, died in August 1954, the business increasingly suffered from what one former employee aptly described as 'the substitution of Engineers, Craftsmen, Motorcyclists and Businessmen by snobs, bookkeepers, whiz kids and paper for work'. As a result, AMC went in little over a decade from being a shining star of the British motorcycle industry to liquidation in 1966. For a short period it was thought that Manganese Bronze and Dennis Poore would continue with the giant Plumstead works, but this did not transpire, and gloom again descended upon the site. The works became derelict and was demolished, the site eventually becoming just another suburban housing estate with not a single surviving feature to recall the organisation that the Colliers and their loyal workforce had striven so hard to build up during the first half of the twentieth century.

Although Manganese Bronze did decide to continue with Norton (successfully launching the new Commando series), together with the AJS

Opposite: Introduced at the London Earls Court Show in November 1964, the Velocette 200cc Vogue was a major sales failure for the Birmingham factory.

The Blackpool Show in May 1963. By then the long-running 350cc Matchless heavyweight single-cylinder (a Mercury is shown here) was well out of date.

Stormer moto-cross bikes and the Wolverhampton-based Villiers engine-manufacturing company (which had also run into financial trouble), Matchless, Francis-Barnett and James were discontinued.

In the summer of 1963 AMC had become the British importers of Suzuki, via a completely new organisation, Suzuki (Great Britain) Ltd; full distribution began later that year. Between October 1963 and October 1964 eighteen thousand of the Japanese machines were imported. This set-up was very much a 'Trojan horse', as Suzuki GB operated from the back door of the James factory in Birmingham.

Well before AMC's demise, the Stevenage-based Vincent concern had failed during the mid-1950s. Vincent's problems were somewhat different, in that they manufactured exclusively specialist machines that were more expensive than their mainstream rivals.

During the early 1960s there had already been signs that the industry was contracting, with BSA closing the Ariel factory in Selly Oak, Birmingham, and moving production to its Small Heath site, while the Norton works in Bracebridge Street, Birmingham, was closed and production relocated to AMC's main factory site in Plumstead, south-east London.

Besides AMC, the other major manufacturing group was BSA (Birmingham Small Arms), which had originally been formed in 1855. The BSA Group evolved over a number of years, with 1910 being a key date for the automotive side, when not only were the first production BSA motorcycles made, but also the Daimler car firm was acquired. In 1919 BSA Cycles was formed (looking after both pedal cycles and motorcycles). In 1928 the Redditch factory (previously used for motorcycle production) closed and all production transferred to Small Heath, Birmingham.

In early 1939, months before the Second World War began, BSA switched to military production. They manufactured a large number of motorcycles for service use, as well as vast quantities of other military equipment. The war years were highly profitable for BSA, enabling the company to make a number of acquisitions, namely Sunbeam (1940), Ariel (1944) and New Hudson (1945). The end of the conflict did not stop BSA acquiring yet more companies, the most important of which was Triumph, purchased in 1951. This, like Ariel, was bought from Jack Y. Sangster. At the same time Sangster joined the BSA board of directors.

The early 1950s were, in motorcycle terms, BSA's golden years, with the company's advertising slogan reflecting this: 'BSA, the most popular motor cycle in the world'. This was certainly true if the sales of Ariel, Triumph, Sunbeam and New Hudson were included.

During this period the BSA Group was a massive organisation producing not simply motorcycles and bicycles, but machine tools, aluminium castings, steel, production cars, buses, heavy engineering and motor vehicle bodies, with British plants not only in Birmingham, but also in Coventry, Sheffield,

One of AMC's last efforts, in 1965, was this factory-produced Matchless G15CSR café racer – essentially a Norton 750 Atlas engine with AMC frame and chaincase, and Norton hubs and forks.

Newcastle-upon-Tyne and London, and subsidiaries in the Irish Republic, France, Canada and the United States.

During the late 1950s, beginning in 1956, several businesses were sold off, examples being the Cycle Division to Raleigh and Daimler Cars to Jaguar Motors.

1960 was the high point in BSA's commercial fortunes, with a record profit of some £3 million. The canny Jack Y. Sangster chose this moment to retire, and from that time the business began a downward spiral. For a start, during the early 1960s the BSA Group was saddled with the twin problems of Edward and Eric Turner, who were not related. The former was the autocratic self-appointed promoter of the Triumph brand, and a designer by then well past his best; among his expensive failures launched in the first half of the 1960s were the Triumph Tina scooter, the BSA Beagle

An experimental Norton P800 double overhead-camshaft parallel twin; it did not get past the prototype stage.

75cc lightweight motorcycle, and the Ariel Pixie 50cc scooterette.

Eric Turner, on the other hand, had become no less of a handicap. Recruited from Blackburn Aircraft, he was essentially an accountant, and so his main purpose in life was cost-cutting. Towards the end of 1963 Edward Turner decided to retire, at the age of sixty-two, but he continued to serve as a consultant.

A major failure from the BSA factory was the 75cc Beagle. It was the work of Edward Turner.

The man chosen to replace him was Harry Sturgeon (then in his early forties), who had previously worked at the de Havilland aircraft factory but had then spent a short period with the Churchill machine tool company, another BSA subsidiary. Unexpectedly, Sturgeon was a success in this new role, and for a few years he got the BSA motorcycle operation back on track. However, the mood of optimism, largely due to Sturgeon's brilliant sales and marketing efforts, particularly in the United States, was not to last, as he developed a brain tumour and, after a long illness, died in April 1967.

Next, another outsider, Lionel Jofeh, arrived in February 1967. Sturgeon's deputy, Bert Hopwood, a gifted engineer and designer, should have succeeded Sturgeon, but Eric Turner (then BSA's chairman) instead recruited Jofeh, head of the Sperry Gyroscopic Company. Although Eric Turner tried to persuade Hopwood to stay, he was not willing to do so.

Rather perversely, the BSA Group won the Queen's Award for Industry in 1967 and again in 1968. But these awards masked what was going on behind the scenes. An example of how bad things were is the development history of the BSA Rocket 3 and Triumph Trident three-cylinder superbikes. These took well over five years to progress from planning to production, not helped by the bitter infighting between BSA and Triumph, largely caused by the efforts of Edward Turner.

In stark contrast to the BSA Beagle, the Triumph T120 Bonneville was a major sales success for the BSA Group.

Lionel Jofeh's appointment was intended to bring in a 'new broom' to BSA, but unfortunately things only got worse, as there was not only a much

A 1966 Triumph Tiger 100 SS. With its 500cc engine size and compact package, it was a popular choice with buyers throughout the 1960s and into the early 1970s.

larger marketing department, but more management consultants, market researchers and, most of all, accountants.

But probably the biggest mistake was Jofeh's personal brainchild, the Research and Development Centre at Umberslade Hall. Purchased by Eric Turner in mid-1967, this was an imposing country mansion at Tamworth-in-Arden, Warwickshire, midway between the Meriden, Small Heath and

The 1971 Triumph T24T Trailblazer – essentially a badge-engined C-series BSA.

Redditch works. It was not fully operational until the end of 1968, when it was run by a staff of three hundred, with an estimated annual cost of £1.5 million. But Umberslade Hall did not solve any problems; it simply created more. For example, it spawned disasters such as the oil-in-frame models, the 50cc Ariel trike, and the 350cc Fury/Bandit twin.

By 1970 BSA was losing vast sums of money and industrial strife was prevalent. After a loss of £8.5 million, Lionel Jofeh parted company with BSA in July 1971; Eric Turner followed in November 1971. Lord Shawcross, a senior executive since 1968, was elected chairman. But all this was far too late; the problems were too big, and the losses too great.

After losing yet more money in the 1972 trading year, the BSA Group neared bankruptcy. The result was a political deal, and takeover by Manganese Holdings, chaired by Dennis Poore, who had already acquired both AMC and Villiers.

The original plan called for Meriden to be shut, and for both Triumph and Norton production to move to Small Heath. But the Meriden workers rebelled and were backed by the new Labour government and its Industry Minister, Tony Benn (Poore had done his original deal with the Conservative government). The last batch of BSAs left Small Heath one evening in the summer of 1973.

The Triumph Workers' Co-operative had come out on top, and attempts to restart production at Small Heath in 1974 failed. This resulted in the vast factory site eventually being sold to the Birmingham Corporation. In 1977 the Small Heath works was demolished. But the Triumph Co-operative's victory was futile in the long run, as it subsequently lost a lot of money from

In 1977 the Meriden Workers' Co-operative produced the Jubilee Bonneville, building one thousand examples as a limited edition in honour of the Silver Jubilee of Queen Elizabeth II.

Velocette were famous for their sporting singles. Leading specialist dealer Geoff Dodkin is seen here with a Thruxton model; in the background is a photograph of the Dodkin Velocette ridden by Tom Phillips. But by the late 1960s this was very much old technology. Velocette ceased production in 1971.

several government handouts over the years and finally closed in 1983. The name alone was sold to a Midlands businessman, John Bloor.

After the Royal Enfield works in Redditch suffered financial troubles in 1967 and closed, limited production of a single model, the 750 Interceptor Mark II, resumed in an underground factory at Bradford-on-Avon, Wiltshire.

So in the end it was Triumph that finally killed off BSA – after the 'management' had tried everything it knew to achieve the same result. It was a sad end to what had been, over the years, Great Britain's largest motorcycle company.

Things were no better for the smaller major British companies, Royal Enfield and Velocette. The former closed its Redditch works in 1967, but relocated to a much smaller facility at Bradford-on-Avon to build the Interceptor 750. The family-owned Velocette concern struggled on until 1971, when it finally ceased production.

FURTHER READING

Bacon, Roy. *British Motorcycles of the 1960s*. Osprey, 1988.

Bacon, Roy. *The British Motorcycle Directory*. The Crowood Press, 2004.

Davies, Ivor. *It's a Triumph*. Haynes, 1980.

Poynting, Roy. *The Sammy Miller Museum Collection: Road Machines*. Redline Books, 2010.

Tratgasch, Erwin. *The New Illustrated Encyclopedia of Motorcycles*. Grange Books, 1993.

Walker, Mick. *Café Racers of the 1960s*. Crowood, 1994.

Walker, Mick. *Café Racers of the 1970s*. Crowood, 2011.

Walker, Mick. *Matchless: The Complete Story*. Crowood, 2004.

Walker, Mick. *Triumph: The Racing Story*. Crowood, 2004.

Walker, Mick. *AJS: The Complete Story*. Crowood, 2005.

Walker, Mick. *BSA Pre-Unit Twins: The Complete Story*. Crowood, 2005.

Walker, Mick. *Motorcycle: Evolution, Design, Passion*. Mitchell Beazley, 2006.

Walker, Mick. *Norton Dominator*. Crowood, 2006.

Walker, Mick. *Velocette: The Racing Story*. Crowood, 2008.

Walker, Mick. *British Motorcycles of the 1940s and '50s*. Shire Publications, 2010.

Wilson, Steve. *British Motorcycles since 1950* (six-volume series). Patrick Stephens, 1982–92.

PLACES TO VISIT

Coventry Transport Museum, Millennium Square, Hales Street, Coventry CV1 1PN. Telephone: 024 7623 4270. Website: www.transport-museum.com A superb display of Coventry-built motorcycles.

Glasgow Transport Museum, 1 Bunhouse Road, Glasgow G3 8DP. Telephone: 0141 287 2720. Website: www.glasgowmuseums.com A wide range of British motorcycles, many in unrestored condition.

National Motor Museum, Beaulieu, Hampshire SO42 7ZN. Telephone: 01590 612345. Website: www.beaulieu.co.uk One of the oldest motor museums; also has a range of motorcycles.

National Motorcycle Museum, Coventry Road, Bickenhill, Solihull, West Midlands B92 0EJ. Telephone: 01675 443311. Website: www.nationalmotorcyclemuseum.co.uk The largest collection of British motorcycles in the world.

Sammy Miller Museum, Bashley Cross Roads, New Milton, Hampshire BH25 5SZ. Telephone: 01425 620777. Website: www.sammymiller.co.uk Magnificent display of road and competition motorcycles, many of which are very rare.

INDEX